MADE

OF

ICELAND

A DRINK & DRAW BOOK

pH powerHouse Books BROOKLYN, NY

Halló from Iceland. You know, that land unlike any other, full of volcanoes, glaciers, geysers, and (the) Northern Lights. We're a culture of inventive spirits, steeped in art, ingenuity, creativity, and a long history of storytelling.

Walking around the city of Reykjavik, where roughly 2/3 of us live, there are stories being told everywhere. From our colorful homes and buildings to the paintings, sketches, folk art, and books that seem to pop up at every turn. In fact, one in ten Icelanders has published a book, more than anywhere else in the world. And once a year we celebrate the national tradition of Jólabókaflóð. This is our "Christmas Book Avalanche" when the majority of books are published and given out as presents.

Of course, stories aren't limited to just being told with words. Just as often, we share stories with pictures. In fact, in a number of bars around here we do something we call "Drink & Draw," where patrons enjoy a cocktail and draw a sketch based on a particular theme. The sketches are then collected and sometimes published in small booklets.

As an Icelandic vodka, you can imagine we're quite fond of this idea. And so we decided to invite a handful of vodka-loving fans to sip a cocktail and doodle whatever their creative spirits desired. The result is this book: A collection of drawings doodled while drinking.

So, pour yourself a cocktail and take a peek. Along the way we'll also share some of the sights, sounds, traditions, and quirks that make our beloved land so unique. From our music and art, to the food, folklore, and natural beauty that make Iceland, well, Iceland.

By the end of this book, hopefully you too will be inspired to grab a pencil and sketch your own interpretation of our homeland. We might even suggest a cocktail or two to compliment your artistic endeavor.

Skál! (That's "cheers" in Icelandic.)

Reyka Vodka
MADE OF ICELAND

Pops!

Eyjafjallajökull
TO
DRAW
Sorry
#CAD0297

MUSIC

OF ICELAND

You can tell a lot about a people by listening to their music. So what does the music of Iceland say about us?

If you showed up before the late 19th century, it may not have said much. Even though we've been making music as far back as ancient times, our own isolation limited our exposure to the influences spreading through Europe. Which meant that for us, the "music of the Middle Ages" lingered well past, shall we say, the middle. But once our ear canals were introduced to a more modern sound, our artistic instincts took hold, and it didn't take long until Icelandic music took on a life of its own. And in recent decades we've proudly shared some acclaimed artists with the world like The Sugarcubes, Björk, Sigur Rós, Gus Gus, Múm, Amiina, and Of Monsters and Men.

Today, our music seems more exploratory, experimental, and artful in nature, rather than being motivated by the search for fame or popularity. The result is a musical culture rich in sonic expansiveness as vast and unique as the landscape we call home.

"Don't think–feel."

Soffía Björg comes from Borgarfjörður, a fjord in the west of Iceland. Studied in classical singing, jazz, bluegrass, and Americana, her experience is as varied as the fjord's undercurrent. Her debut album included fellow Icelandic musicians Ingibjörg Elsa, Kristofer Rodriquez, Pétur Ben, and producer Ben Hillier.

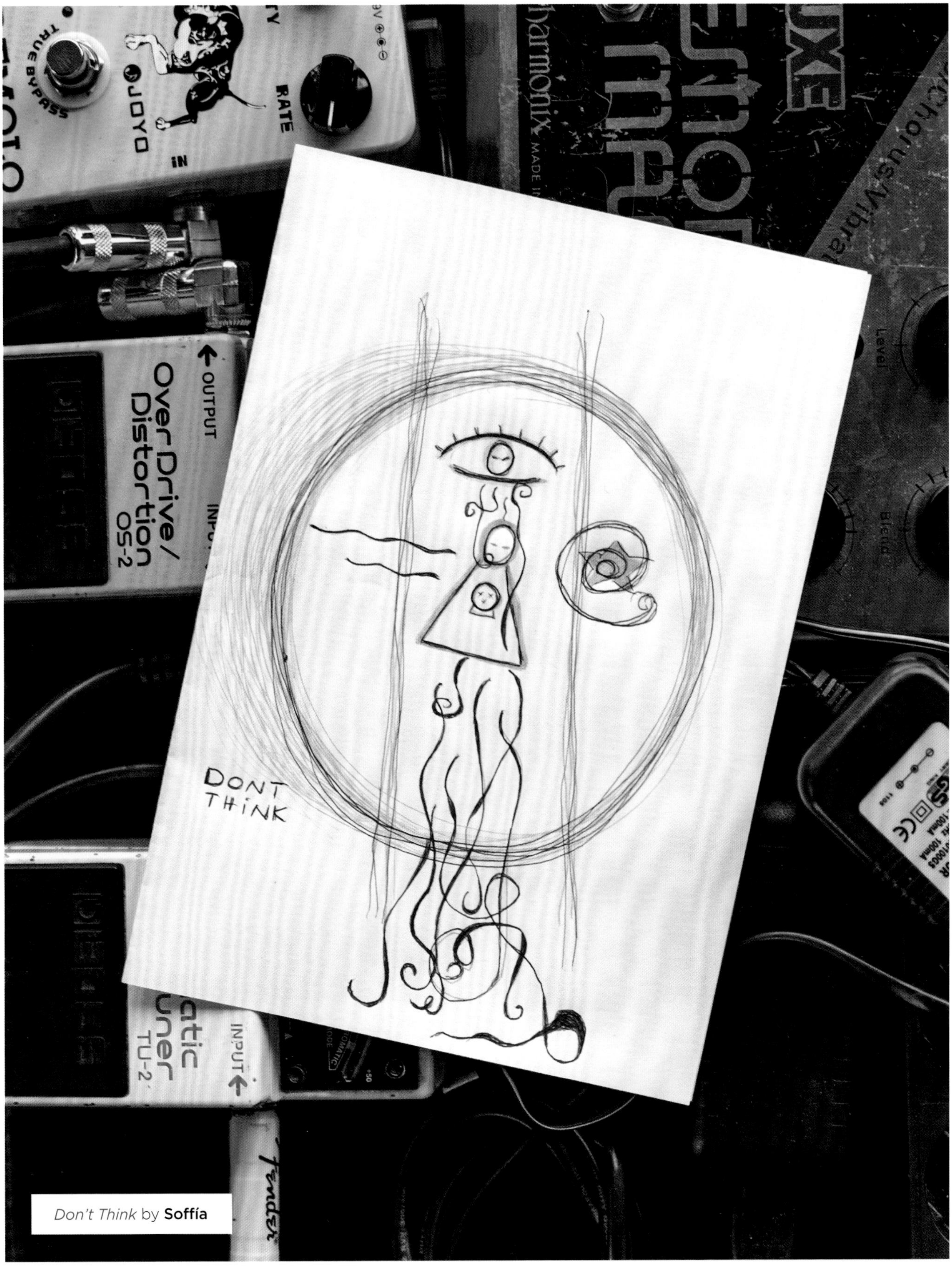

Don't Think by **Soffía**

Puffin
bartender

BARTENDER WITH FISH SWIMMING SHIRT
TO DRAW

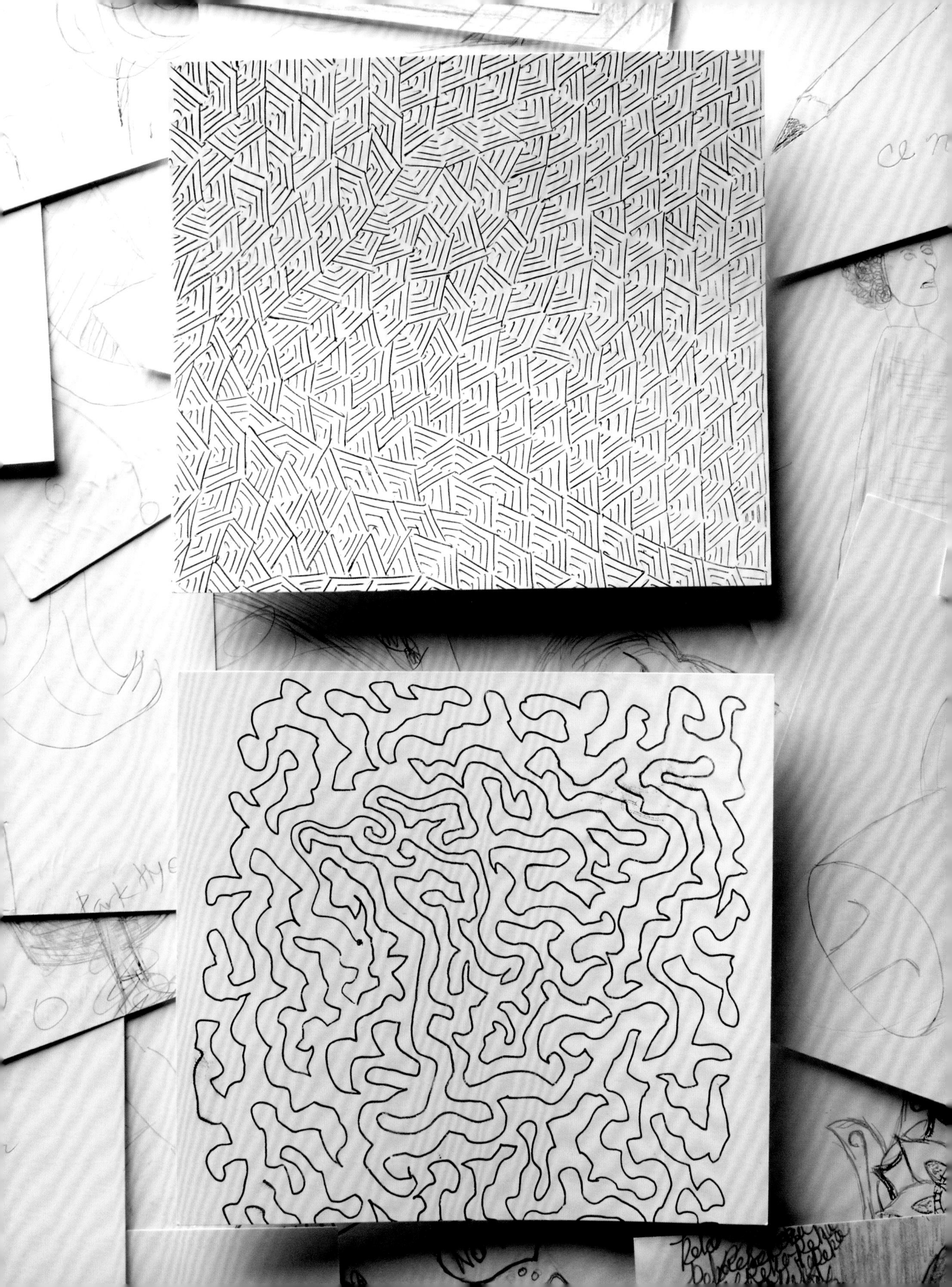

REYKA

THIS IS A DOODLE OF MY BEST FRIEND!
TAKK!
THIS IS A DOODLE OF MY BEST FRIEND WITH HIS BEST FRIEND...

CUISINE

OF ICELAND

Odds are you don't have a favorite neighborhood Icelandic place, but that doesn't mean Icelandic cuisine is to be ignored. At first blush, it's easy to write off our traditional foods of the past as, well, foods of the past.

Ancient Icelandic recipes like cod cheeks, fermented shark, singed sheep heads, blood pudding, liver sausages, and dried fish rarely make the list of modern foodie favorites. But it would be a mistake to judge Icelandic cuisine on the hand-to-mouth farming practices of the past.

Contemporary Icelandic cuisine actually rivals most Western nations, with chefs taking full advantage of our pure, natural landscape to create inspired dishes worthy of recognition on the global stage. From produce grown in 100% sustainable geothermal greenhouses, to free-range animals raised on grasses free of hormones or pesticides, modern Icelandic chefs are striking culinary gold thanks to the benefits of our supernatural terrain.

Today, popular artisanal staples like breads, cheeses, beers, tea, and sea salts are a proud part of our edible output, more so than our ancient traditional meals. So if your neighborhood is indeed lacking an Icelandic joint, we say it's well overdue for a change.

“Icelandic wool sweaters, beer, food, arts, design, music. All things made of Iceland inspire me, as do interesting people, angling, hunting, hiking, foraging, and swimming in Icelandic nature.”

Óli is a straightforward country boy from the eastern part of Iceland who has made more than a name for himself as an innovative chef in Reykjavík. Thriving in environments where creativity is just as important as keeping cool under pressure, he has found his unique place in the culinary world.

Heart by **Óli**

REYKA
I'D RATHER BE SKÅL-ING

miles

REYKA

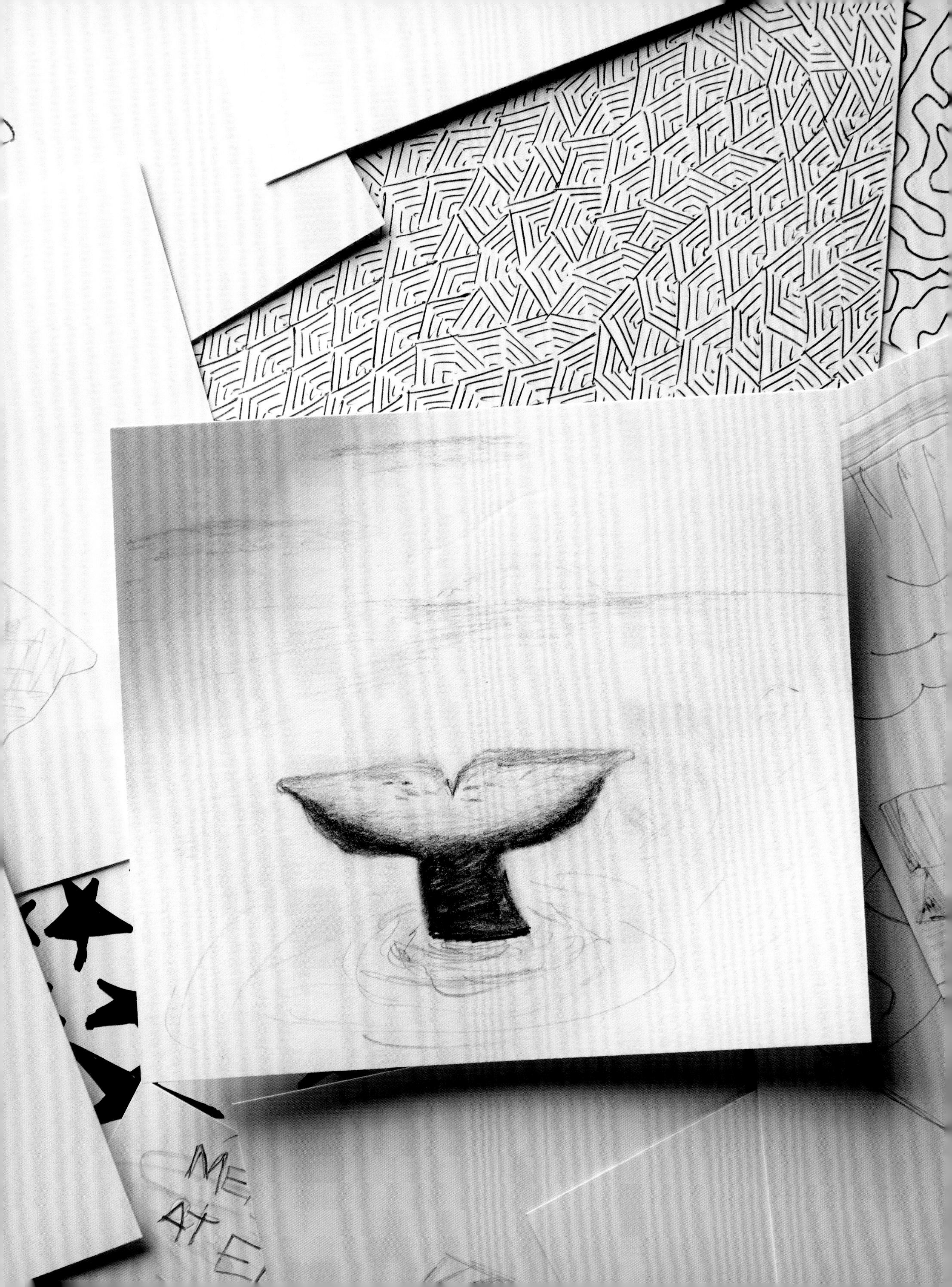

FASHION

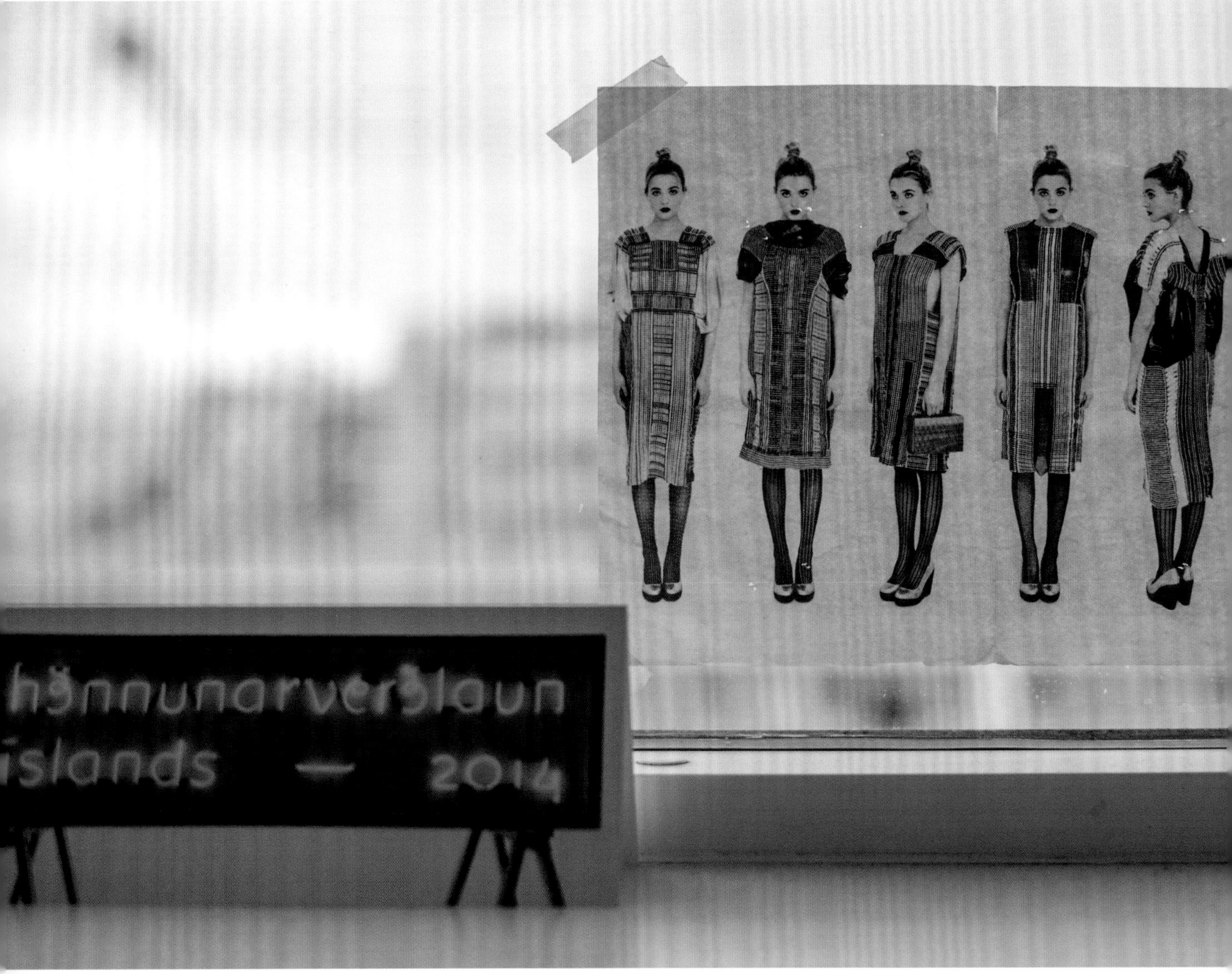

OF ICELAND

To most of the world, Icelanders are traditionally thought of as being a little off-beat and quirky. Which suits us just fine. And speaking of suits, a big part of that perception probably comes from our fashion sense. While we traditionally embrace minimalistic designs, and layers, of course, we're a place that encourages you to embrace your own personal style. Simple. Eclectic. Western. Truly original. It's all a welcome sight on the sidewalks of Reykjavik.

For fashion designers there's certainly no lack of creative inspiration in our country. And when it comes to clothing, we don't have any deep-rooted traditions, other than making sure we stay warm. And that general lack of grounding actually works to our advantage guaranteeing freedom and creativity for the styles being created year after year.

Our fashion industry is relatively young, but booming. And it takes a certain amount of pride in its smallness. There's a unique sense of togetherness within the design community that you won't find in other fashion meccas like New York or London. Budding designers and entrepreneurs take joy in working together to make the creative community stronger as a whole.

By the way, in case you were wondering, that classic Icelandic sweater that we're sort of known for is called lopapeysa. If you ever come for a visit, you should definitely pick one up. They're super cozy.

“It is important for me to embrace my heritage by sourcing local materials to create something new.”

Magnea Einarsdottir is the founder of MAGNEA, a creative fashion studio based in Reykjavík. MAGNEA is known for innovative knitwear. Inspired by everything and nothing, Magnea’s aim is to use traditional methods in an unseen way.

Wool by **Magnea**

LAND HO!

Thinking
AND
Drinking
in
NYC

BAR

REYKA

Góðan dag

— MY NEW
HAIR=EWE

ART AND DESIGN

OF ICELAND

When you consider the entire history of Iceland, visual artistry is a relatively new achievement for us. For the longest time our creative and cultural output was literary. But in the last century or so, our art scene has come on strong. These days, it's absolutely thriving. And not just here. So many Icelandic artists are world-renown and have put on acclaimed exhibits the world over, from New York City to Frankfurt to Tokyo.

The most dominant force in Icelandic art is usually considered to be our landscape. Can you blame us? It's an endless source of inspiration, and artists are constantly finding creative ways to interpret it.

When it comes to design, Icelanders are known for our ingenuity and distinct style. At times, our sensibilities are similar to that of traditional Scandinavian minimalism. But we're always trying to push the limits of form, function, color, and material. Much like our art, our design is inspired by the breathtaking nature all around us. Our eco-consciousness also plays a major role, giving us strong roots in recycling and repurposing of objects as much as possible.

All of that adds up to an aesthetic approach that reflects our quirky sensibilities and the natural drama of our country. It's a style that can only be described as truly Icelandic.

“Mother earth is holy. She gives me life and humanity and centers me. In gratitude I return my art. Love and peace.”

Þorlákur Kristinsson (Tolli) emerged as one of the instigators of the New Painting Movement in the early 1980s. An eruption of emotion and push-back against over-analysis and excessive rationality in the arts, few artistic movements swept aside so many adherents in such a short time.

The Meditator by **Tolli**

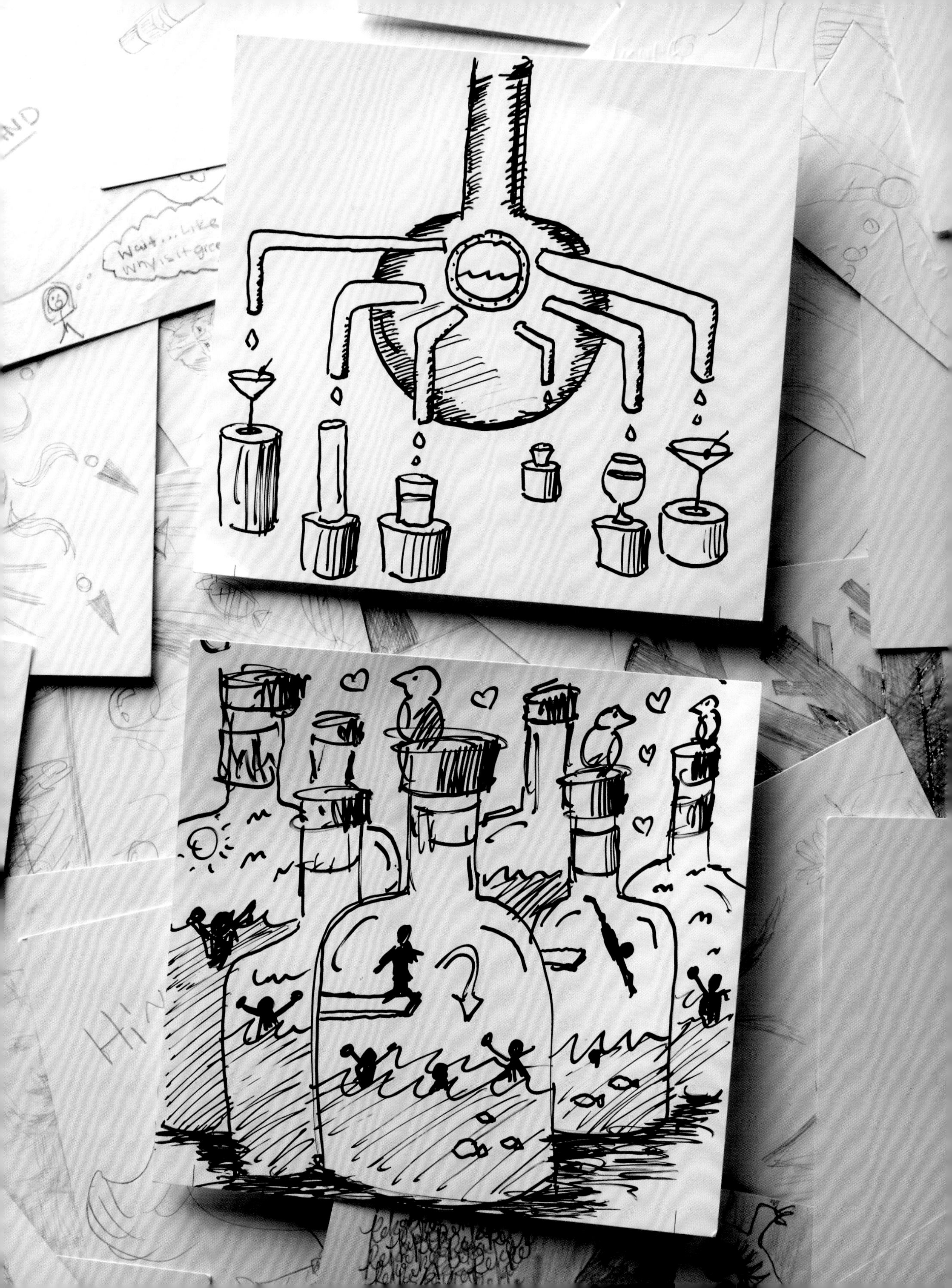
Wait... Like

REYKA
VODKA
Copi 16
ICE LAN
Polar B
ne sont
crayon

I'm very OPEN MINDED...

Now it's time to pick up a pen or pencil and draw your own creation. Why not try sketching your own interpretation of what it means to be MADE OF ICELAND? If you like your creation, feel free to post it with the hashtag #madeoficeland. We just might reach out and say hello. To do it like we do in Iceland, here are a few cocktail suggestions to accompany your creative endeavors, which we have no doubt, will be magnificent.

Basil Collins

Spicy Palmer Tea

Icelandic Mule

Solstice Punch

BASIL COLLINS

1 ½ parts Reyka Vodka
¾ part lemon juice
½ part simple syrup
Club soda
2-4 Basil leaves

GLASS: Collins
GARNISH: Basil leaf
METHOD: Shake

Combine all ingredients in a cocktail shaker, except soda. Shake, double strain into glass, top with soda, garnish and serve.

SPICY PALMER TEA

1 ½ parts Reyka Vodka
1 part Ancho Reyes Chile Liqueur
¾ part fresh lemon juice
6 parts unsweetened iced tea

GARNISH: Lemon wheel
GLASS: Collins
METHOD: Shake

Combine all ingredients into cocktail shaker. Shake, garnish, and serve.

ICELANDIC MULE

2 parts Reyka Vodka
1 part ginger beer
2 parts apple cider
¼ part simple syrup

GLASS: Mule cup
GARNISH: Cinnamon stick & apple slice
METHOD: Shake

Combine all ingredients in a cocktail shaker, except ginger beer. Shake, double strain into glass, add ginger beer, garnish, and serve.

SOLSTICE PUNCH

1 part Reyka Vodka
½ part Solerno Blood Orange Liqueur
½ part fresh lemon juice
½ part vanilla simple syrup
½ part pomegranate juice (POM)
½ part sparkling water

GLASS: Punch glass
GARNISH: Mint sprig

vanilla syrup: combine equal parts sugar and water and shake. For every 24 oz., add .5 oz. vanilla extract.

Combine all ingredients together in a cocktail shaker and shake/strain. Garnish with mint sprig.

YOUR MEISTARAVERK (THAT'S "MASTERPIECE" IN ICELANDIC) **HERE**

SHARE YOUR DRAWING ON SOCIAL MEDIA WITH #MADEOFICELAND

YOUR MEISTARAVERK (THAT'S "MASTERPIECE" IN ICELANDIC) HERE

SHARE YOUR DRAWING ON SOCIAL MEDIA WITH #MADEOFICELAND

ABOUT REYKA

Iceland is a land of volcanoes and glaciers, with fields of lava rock as far as the eye can see and towering waterfalls of pure spring water. It's a land unlike any other. So it's no surprise that Icelanders have an interesting view of the world.

When Reyka Vodka set out to distill the best tasting vodka in the world, we took inspiration from the country's natural resources and the inventive spirit that make this island and its people so charmingly offbeat.

We start with Iceland's glacial spring water, which is some of the purest water in the world. It's what gives Reyka its crisp, clean taste. Then we use lava rocks as a natural and oh-so-efficient filtration system. Lava rocks have zero tolerance for impurities and are conveniently located in our many lava rock fields. Then we distill our vodka in a rare Carter-Head Still which further increases it's purity. It's the first and only one of its kind used to distill vodka. This process, and our entire distillery, are powered by the steam from underground hot springs. This geo-thermal energy supplies power without adding contaminates to our vodka. Or the world.

The Reyka distillery is located 74 km outside of Reykjavik, in a coastal village called Borgarnes. We craft our vodka in preciously small batches to make sure every bottle is of the highest quality. The final result is a vodka that's exceptionally smooth and rounded with a soft, natural sweetness. A slight hint of wild fruits is balanced with a crisp and silky finish. We think that sometimes all you need is Reyka with a little ice and a dash of bitters, but we've also included some of our favorite simple recipes in this book a few pages back.

We like to say that Reyka isn't just made in Iceland. It's made of Iceland. With all the unique qualities and characteristics that make our island unlike any other place on Earth.

We hope you'll enjoy a sip soon.

Learn more about us at Reyka.com

ABOUT SNORRI STURLUSON

The book's creative direction and oversight was provided by Snorri Sturluson. A creative professional who's worked in the arts all his life, Snorri started as a music photographer in Iceland in the 80s where his first collaborators were Kukl (Björk's pre-Sugarcubes band). His images from that time are frequently seen in books chronicling the early days of the now world-renowned Icelandic music scene. In the 90s Snorri was a music executive at several Icelandic music labels and a founding member of Mr. Destiny which started the Iceland Airwaves Music Festival.

In 2001, Snorri moved to New York where he has been working as a creative director, photographer, and director for many of the world's top ad agencies and their clients. His talent has increasingly brought him behind a film camera as a director and he has spearheaded hundreds of commercials, VR experiences, music videos, and branded content campaigns. His work has been featured at the highest level, such as the Super Bowl, The Oscars, NFL Kickoff Night, and festivals around the world, where it's garnered awards and accolades for clients such as BMW, Mercedes Benz, Verizon, Apple, Chrysler, and many more.

Snorri continues to work on a lot of cross-creative projects, developing unique content in collaboration with brands and agencies across disciplines ranging from digital to film to print to VR and beyond.

LITERACY PARTNERS

Reading and creative freedom are so important to Iceland that Reyka will be donating all proceeds from this book to Literacy Partners.

Literacy Partners is dedicated to empowering parents by providing the highest quality English-language education to families in New York, NY. The organization's goal is to strengthen families and reduce poverty through a two-generation approach to literacy instruction that encompasses parenting skills, health, financial literacy, and job readiness.

Together with their students, they strive to close the achievement gap for children before they even begin school.

To learn more about Literacy Partners and their dedication to offering high quality, community-based literacy programs, visit www.literacypartners.org.

ICELAND NATURALLY

Iceland Naturally is a cooperative marketing organization that promotes the services, products, and culture of Iceland. Through events, promotions, and online marketing initiatives, Iceland Naturally introduces Iceland's creativity and natural wonders to North Americans. The group is comprised of Iceland's top companies and organizations: Reyka Vodka, Icelandair, Icelandic Group, Islandsbanki, City of Reykjavik, Icelandic Glacial Water, Blue Lagoon, Keflavik International Airport (KEF), Landsvirkjun, Ölgerðin Egill Skallagrímsson, Promote Iceland, and the Government of Iceland. www.icelandnaturally.com

ACKNOWLEDGMENTS

Special thanks to everyone involved
in the creation of this book
and the cocktails consumed along the way.

William Grant & Sons

Curich | Weiss

Red Tettemer O'Connell + Partners

Momentum Worldwide NA

Page One Public Relations

Iceland Naturally

Sturla Þengilsson

Tómas Sturluson

Kári Sturluson

And of course, to the countless number of creative
people who participated in Reyka Drink & Draw
events or submitted their drawings.

MADE OF ICELAND:

A Drink & Draw Book

Please drink Reyka responsibly. Takk! (That's "thank you" in Icelandic.)
Reyka Vodka, 40% Alc/Vol. (80 Proof) Distilled from Grain.

Published in the United States by powerHouse Books,
a division of powerHouse Cultural Entertainment, Inc.
37 Main Street, Brooklyn, NY 11201-1021
telephone 212.604.9074, fax 212.366.5247
e-mail: info@powerHouseBooks.com
website: www.powerHouseBooks.com

First edition, 2016

Library of Congress Control Number: 2016947493

Hardcover ISBN 978-1-57687-832-3

Printing and binding by Asia Pacific Offset

Book design by Krzysztof Poluchowicz
Art direction by Snorri Sturluson

10 9 8 7 6 5 4 3 2 1

Printed and bound in China